The Return of TRY THIS ONE

IDEAS FOR YOUTH GROUPS

Edited by Cindy S. Hansen
Designed by Judy Atwood
Illustrations by Martin Bucella

Loveland, CO 80539

Selected from the regular feature "Try This One"
in GROUP, the youth ministry magazine

The Return of
TRY THIS ONE

First Printing

Library of Congress Cataloging-in-Publication Data

The Return of . . . try this one.

   "Selected from the regular feature "Try this
one" in Group, the youth ministry magazine."
   1. Church group work with youth—Hand-
books, manuals, etc.   I. Hansen, Cindy S.
BV4447   1986   259'.2   86-14252
ISBN 0-931529-13-1 (pbk.)

Printed in the United States of America

CONTENTS

Group Growth Goodies

Fun Fund Raisers

INTRODUCTION

Since the birth of **GROUP** Magazine in 1974, "Try This One" has been one of the magazine's most popular features. "Try This One" lists the latest and greatest activities used by Christian youth group members and leaders from all over the country. No wonder it's so popular!

The Return of Try This One is the fifth collection of ideas from "Try This One" in **GROUP**. Use this handy resource to meet your group members' needs. For example:

● **the need to have fun!** The "Fun 'n' Games" section is filled with creative crowdbreakers, games, parties and special events to liven up your group.

● **the need to grow as a group.** The "Group Growth Goodies" section helps kids grow together as well as reach out to others.

● **the ever-present need to raise funds.** The "Fun Fund Raisers" section offers a treasure chest full of profit-making ventures. The fund raisers focus on community-building and helping others as well as replenishing your youth fund.

Be daring! Use the ideas listed here and have fun with them. Be creative! Adapt, modify and enlarge the activities to fit your specific needs.

Be an author! Write down new ideas that work well with your youth group—and send them to us. See "Your Ideas Wanted" on page 79 for more details.

Fun 'n' Games

BALLOON HUNT

You'll get a BANG out of this activity. Get two or more teams and lots of balloons (at least three per group member). The hunt works best in a building with several rooms.

Assign each team a headquarters room. Then give the instructions and five minutes to get organized. During that five minutes, group sponsors randomly disperse balloons throughout the building.

The instructions each team receives:
1. Your team colors are red, green and yellow (or whatever).
2. You are to "rescue" all balloons of your team colors and take them to your headquarters for safekeeping.
3. You may pop an opposing team's balloons by using your feet only.
4. You may not enter an opposing team's headquarters.

Give each team the same number of balloons to be rescued.

On your signal, the hunt begins. The team with the most rescued balloons wins. For a quick and competitive cleanup, have a Dead Balloon Hunt: Teams race through the building finding unfortunate balloon victims of any color. The team bringing in the most popped balloons wins.

—Larry Walton, Roseburg, Oregon

BODY PARTS

Here's a good discussion starter for devotions on 1 Corinthians 12:12-31.

Cover an open doorway with butcher paper. In the center, cut a hole that is 3 inches in diameter.

Divide group members into teams of three or four. Send one team at a time behind the door. Tell the team members to, one at a time, each place a different body part up to the hole. Instruct the other teams to write down what they think each part is, and who it belongs to (for example, Sally's ear, Joe's elbow, Pete's tongue).

Your group members will discover how hard it is to pick out a person by one part. Emphasize that this is how it is with the body of Christ: We are all parts in that body, but it is hard to be recognized as a witness in the world if only one part (person) is being seen.

Our discussion of 1 Corinthians 12:12-31 after this game was out of sight!

—Scott Welch, Wilmore, Kentucky

BOUNDARY BALL

It's as much fun to lose as it is to win in this action-packed ball game.

You'll need: an outside wall with space in front of it, a bouncy soccer-size ball, a rope and a "referee."

Use the rope to mark off a large square boundary, with the wall serving as one side. All players stand inside the boundary and begin throwing the ball against the wall. Players must avoid being hit by the rebounding ball before it bounces.

A player who is hit by the ball is "out" and must become part of the boundary by standing on the rope. The boundary-people catch and return the ball—just as the wall does—and if the rebounding ball hits an active player before it bounces, that player is also
"out" and must join the boundary-people.

The referee may periodically shout, "Boundary, take one step in." This makes it more difficult for the active players to dodge the rebounding ball.

Award your winner—the last active player—with a bouncy ball signed by all the other group members.

—Dennis Henn, Wenatchee, Washington

BROWNIE TASTE TEST

Here's an idea that's fun and involves both young people and adults from your congregation.

Announce in your church newsletter or bulletin that your youth group is conducting a Brownie Taste Test at their next meeting. Ask church members to submit a batch of their favorite brownies to include in the test. Include the time, place and date for delivery. Make sure each batch is labeled with the name, address and telephone number of the baker.

The kids will love the taste feast and the cooks will love showing off. Send thank-you notes to all entrants and a special note to the winner.

—Suzanne Rushworth, Hixson, Tennessee

CAPTION WRITERS

As you look through magazines and newspapers, you often can find humorous pictures, which are sometimes even funnier if you remove the captions underneath.

So get the creative juices flowing and laughs abounding. Put up a captionless picture in the youth room or church hallway each week. Give youth group members several days to write in their own funny captions. If you want to make it competitive, have members judge the best

caption and award a prize to the winner. But you'll likely find the incentive of a prize isn't necessary to get teenagers involved in this creative caption exercise.

—Scott Welch, Athens, Georgia

CHASE THAT GOOSE

Once you try this activity, you'll end up doing it every year. You can do this on foot in the summer or by car in the winter.

The goal is to find the person in town with the live goose (or duck or chicken) in a crate in his or her car. Find a farmer who's willing to let you borrow a goose for an afternoon or evening—maybe even once a year for this activity as the "youth group mascot."

Write creative treasure-hunt-type clues. Write enough clues for two teams, but have only the last clues (saying where the goose is) be the same. We use six clues for each team. Place the clues around town (for example, with a gas station attendant, or in a phone booth).

Divide group members into two teams. Give both teams their first clues and say that the first team back with the honking crate wins. Once they're back, have a goose-wrapping contest! Remind everyone to be gentle with the goose. Let the first team take wrapping paper and ribbons and wrap the goose. Take a photo with an instant-print camera. Then the second team wraps the goose. Take a photo, then judge the two. Our kids have so much fun with this that they hurt from laughing.

Wrap up the time together with a discussion on what things in life lead us on a wild-goose chase, and how Jesus can give direction to life.

—Steve Bolda, Waupun, Wisconsin

CLONE PARTY

Use this "backdoor" approach to emphasize each youth group member's special uniqueness: Have a Clone Party!

When you publicize the party, distribute a list of requirements for attendance: Everyone must wear non-signature blue jeans, a white shirt, a white sock on the left foot and a black one on the right, tennis shoes, and no jewelry; everyone must chew gum; etc.

Tailor games to the "everyone do the same thing the same way" idea.

At snack time, instruct your "clones" to eat using their left hands only.

At some point, have group members get into small groups and list things they have in common (for example: use the same brand of toothpaste; play the same sport; like the same type of music; shower in the morning; etc.).

CLONE PARTY

Then as a whole group, discuss the lists and why they are so short. Emphasize that no matter how much we try to conform, we can't escape the fact that God created each of us **differently.**

Close your Clone Party with a devotion from 1 Corinthians 12 about how each person is unique and special in God's eyes.

—Alton R. Noblett, Caldwell, Texas

DOG BISCUIT RELAY

This hilarious relay is great for any size group.

If your group is large, divide kids into teams of five or more players. If your group is small, divide into two teams and repeat the relay two or more times to determine the winning team.

Have each team form a straight line with each team member down on all fours (like a dog) facing forward.

Give group members each a pinch-type clothespin to put in their mouth so the clothespin can be opened and closed with their teeth.

Put bowls with 10 to 12 dog biscuits in each on the floor in front of each team's line. The first person in each team's line must take the dog biscuits out of the bowl, one at a time, using the clothespin in their mouth. The biscuits are then passed on to the next person, and so on down the line.

If a biscuit is dropped, the person who dropped it must pick it up with the clothespin. No hands are allowed at any time.

Teams must stay in a straight line and remain on hands and knees throughout the relay.

The first team to put all its biscuits in the bowl at the end of the line wins.

—Steve Wilfert, Merrimack, New Hampshire

DO-IT-YOURSELF MINIATURE GOLF

Here's an activity you can do either indoors or outdoors.

Do-It-Yourself Miniature Golf plays like croquet, with hoops instead of holes. Use coat hangers to make hoops (indoors, secure them with masking tape; outdoors, stick them into the ground).

Divide group members into several small groups and give each group its hoop and a variety of raw materials such as cardboard boxes, large pieces of Styrofoam, packing materials, scrap wood, building blocks, rope. Explain that each group is responsible to design one hole of the course. Assign the groups adjacent areas, and announce the amount of time they have to complete their "hole."

To play, use croquet balls and mallets, or tennis balls and hockey sticks. Rotate the small groups from hole to hole, having them keep their score. The winning group has the least total number of tries to get the balls through all the hoops.

My youth group loves this!

—Jeffrey Collins, Lexington, Massachusetts

DON'T BLOW IT

This activity is great at parties.

You'll need two medium-sized candles with candle holders, matches, string, soft-drink bottle caps and a sharp utensil for punching holes in the bottle caps.

Divide your group members into two teams. Let each team choose its own name (name ideas: Dr. Pepper Team; The Coca-Colas; Pepsi Generation). Poke a hole in the middle of each bottle cap. Thread a string through the hole, knotting it underneath. Cut the string long enough to fit around a person's waist so the bottle cap dangles about one foot from the floor.

Place the two candles on the floor a short distance from the teams. Light the candles and explain the game: On a "go" command each person, one at a time, is to slowly back up to one candle. Have kids each bend down and with their bottle cap try extinguishing the candle without using their hands. Once the flame is out, they race back to their team members and another person tries to put out the flame. Note: Have a person ready to light the candles after they've been extinguished.

Serve soft drinks afterward.

—Jim and Mershon Shrigley, Schaumburg, Illinois

GEORGE

This variation of a familiar game will keep your kids thinking.

Have group members sit on chairs in a circle. Remove any empty chairs. Everyone should tell his or her first name (if there are duplicates, use last names), except for the leader. The leader gives his or her name as "George."

The object of the game is to unseat George. The play begins: George alternately claps hands and knees to set up a rhythm, which the group follows and maintains. To the beat of the rhythm, George then says "George" and the name of another person in the circle. The person whose name George called must repeat his or her own name and add someone else's without missing a beat, and so on.

George determines when someone "messes up" by (1) breaking the rhythm or (2) calling the name of the person who just called on him or her. When someone goofs, that person must move to the "last" seat in the circle—the seat at George's left. Then other group members move clockwise to fill in the seats.

Now, the fun: When people move to new seats, they acquire new names because each chair keeps the name of the first person who sat in it. So every time a group member shifts to a new seat, he or she should ask the person leaving it "What's the name of this chair?" That way he or she will know which name to respond to.

The game ends when George goofs—determined unanimously by everyone else. If you choose to continue playing, George moves one seat to the left, causing everyone to change seats. The new person in the George seat becomes "George" and all other chairs acquire the names of the group members now sitting in them.

—Rhett G. Payne III, Marshall, Texas

HIGH-TECH SLIDES

Here's a quick and easy way to use personal computers to make sing-along or announcement slides with excellent graphics. You'll need a personal computer with word-processing software and a 35mm single-lens reflex camera.

Simply type into the computer the words you want so that on the screen they look exactly like you want the slide to look. Take a picture of the screen: Use a tripod to steady the camera, and artificial light (for example, a strobe). Set the shutter speed to 1/60 second, and use standard 64- or 100-ASA slide film.

With a little imagination, you'll be making creative, high-tech slides in no time.

—Ben Sharpton, Kissimmee, Florida

JUNKMANIA

Set aside an afternoon your kids will remember for a long time: Have a Junkmania!

Get permission from a junkyard owner to take your group to the junkyard. Also take along a tool kit with various tools. Tell group members they have three hours in which to

build the wildest contraptions they can. Some kids may form teams; some may prefer to work alone; but, if your group is like mine, everyone will need the three hours!

After the time limit, as a whole group travel from spot to spot and examine each invention. Have the creators explain what they are for and demonstrate how they work.

Give awards for the biggest, the weirdest and the most usable inventions, as well as for the dirtiest and cleanest team or persons!

You also could have a brief devotion on 2 Corinthians 5:17, highlighting the fact that in Christ we are new creations; the old becomes new.

If the weather is warm enough, take your group swimming in a nearby lake to wash up.

—Scott Welch, North East, Maryland

NEWSLETTER PIZZA CONTEST

Do you ever wonder whether your teenagers read the youth group newsletter?

I did, so I decided to create a contest to challenge them to read it for typing errors. The first 10 who find a typo in the monthly newsletter win a free pizza meal with their youth minister. I use my answering machine to get an accurate "first 10" count.

This works well for many reasons:

● The kids **do** read the newsletters now.

● Going out for pizza with the kids helps me get to know them better.

● Going out for pizza also helps 10 diverse kids get to know each other better.

● It keeps me humble; the kids find more errors than I

plan.

I'm thinking of having Bible quiz questions next.

—Terry Caouette, Duluth, Minnesota

NIGHT OF THE LEPRECHAUN

Try this one for St. Patrick's Day fun.

Before the meeting, tell group members to bring Leprechaun "bait" from home (for example, Lucky Charms, parsley, peas, potatoes, green M&M's).

Meet at the church and say, "Now is your chance to catch a Leprechaun and receive a pot of gold."

Have group members form teams of three. Ask the teams to create the Leprechaun traps from materials in the church such as paper bags, string, nursery cribs and coffee cans. "Bait" the traps and have another sponsor take the young people to another room to play games. (This allows the Leprechaun time to find the goodies.)

By the most creative trap, leave a bag of gold (chocolate candies wrapped in gold foil) and the following Leprechaun message: "Thought you could catch me, did you now? Better luck next year. Enjoy the gold anyhow!"

After a few minutes, gather the members and let them discover the message and pot of gold. Serve refreshments such as peppermint ice cream, lemon-lime soda with green food coloring, shamrock-shaped cookies or mushroom pizza.

As a finishing touch, sing St. Patrick's Day carols: "O Leprechaun, O Leprechaun . . ."

—John Skelly, Blaine, Minnesota

100 PERCENT CHANCE OF RAIN

This setting-priorities exercise works well with both junior highers and senior highers. We call it 100 Percent Chance of Rain.

The publicity reads: "Imagine you are Noah. You know it's going to rain for 40 days and 40 nights. You also know that dams will burst, rivers will overflow, sewers will back up—the Earth will be covered with water. God tells you that he'll permit only you and a few others to board the Royal Princess.

"Space is a major restriction on the Royal Princess. You may bring along only what you can carry in your arms.

"What will you bring with you? Think about it this week. Bring those items to the meeting (give date, place, time).

"We'll talk about what we brought with us and why. (If you can't bring something, like a water bed, bring a picture or a drawing of the item.)"

The variety of items kids bring to this meeting is always wide: stuffed and real animals, stereos, a baby sister. This activity prompts enthusiastic discussion about our priorities and the end of the world.

—Gary N. McCluskey, Colorado Springs, Colorado

ONE, TWO, BUCKLE MY SHOE

Here's a simple but fun game that's popular in our group.

Have the kids sit in a circle, take off their shoes and pile them in the middle. Then blindfold two or three group members at a time, spin them around three times and send them in the direction of the shoes. Each person tries to find his or her own shoes

first and put them on. Once a person has put on the shoes, he or she may remove the blindfold. Many times the members discover they've put on two different shoes! After taking a turn, each member puts his or her shoes back in the pile.

It's so much fun we usually continue by having the winners of each round compete three at a time until we end up with a grand champion.

—Sherry Westergard, Dagmar, Montana

PLUNGER RELAY

Here's a hilarious variation for your next set of relay games.

You'll need a beach towel and a toilet plunger for each team, plus masking tape and a non-carpeted floor.

Make a circle on the floor with masking tape for your starting line and place an object in the center for a "touch base." Divide your group into equal teams of three or more players. Arrange the teams like spokes of a wheel outside the starting line facing the center.

Give each team a beach towel and toilet plunger. At the signal one person from each team sits cross-legged on the towel and uses the plunger as an oar to push his or her team's "boat" to the center.

The player must touch the base then push the boat back to the outside of the circle where the next team member repeats the process.

Try this relay in the snow or mud using a plastic garbage bag for the boat. Yuck, what a mess! Get ready for lots of laughs no matter where you try this one.

—Ronda Ary, Kearney, Missouri

PUTTING ON THE GOSPEL HITS

Why not try your own version of Putting on the Hits, the television show where air bands compete for prizes? Here's an idea we did, called Putting on the **Gospel** Hits, using contemporary Christian music in a lip-sync contest.

Plan a special contest night and invite church members and friends. Select a few judges and score each contestant or air band. Use this point system:

Area	Top Score
Originality	30 points
Appearance	30 points
Lip-sync	30 points

Give Christian concert tickets or a popular Christian album as an award for the best act (whoever scores the most points).

Let young people briefly tell about the song they chose to perform. Have them stress the importance of the words or message it portrays.

—Tom Bronson, Elkland, Pennsylvania

SOCK SOCCER

This simple "soccer" game is a favorite in our group.

The basic rules of soccer remain the same; the field, ball and footgear are altered.

The field is approximately 25 feet wide by 40 feet long, with a chair at each end for goals.

Players take off their shoes and play in their socks, and they use an old tennis ball instead of a soccer ball.

Even out-of-shape sponsors and members enjoy this ridiculous game! All the members are laughing and exhausted when they quit.

—Phil McCraw, Cedar Park, Texas

SQUAWKER VOLLEYBALL

If you want to liven up a dreary day, Squawker Volleyball is just what you need.

Go to a store that sells birthday party supplies. Purchase several "squawker" balloons; they make a horrendous noise as air slowly escapes from them.

Set up a volleyball net and have teams volley a squawking, deflating balloon back and forth across the net. The team that ends up with the fully deflated balloon on its side loses the point.

Make sure the activity doesn't take place the same time as a prayer meeting!

—Andy Britt, Sylvania, Georgia

STAFF TRIVIA

This game will appeal to your group members' love of trivia, and also better acquaint them with the youth group adult staff—sponsors, leaders, pastor, etc. Make sure all the adults who help with the group attend.

Begin by having group members write questions for the following four trivia categories. Some sample questions are, for sports and leisure: What's your favorite hobby?; for science and nature: How do you like your eggs prepared? What color best describes you in the morning?; for entertainment: What's your favorite TV show?; for arts and literature: Which of the seven dwarfs in **Snow White and the Seven Dwarfs** best describes you?

Divide group members into teams of equal numbers, and assign each team a staff member. The teams will compete to correctly answer the most questions about their staff members.

As you ask each question, the staff members must write their answers while the team members confer and then produce their best guess. Award three points for each team's correct answer; keep score.

For variety, put a few group members rather than adults on the hot seat.

—Mark Seanor, West Monroe, Louisiana

SUMMER DREAMING

There's nothing like dreaming of summer to beat the winter doldrums. Our group combined "summer dreaming" with summer planning and had a great time.

We publicized Summer Dreaming three weeks in advance and announced that group members should come dressed in summer gear.

We decorated the meeting hall with beach blankets, umbrellas, summer posters, and surfboards. We played the Beach Boys' **Endless Summer** album in the background.

Group members arrived dressed as though it were summer; some even had on suntan lotion. We gave prizes for the "coolest" and for the best winter tan (the whitest skin).

Games included a surfing pantomime contest and Beach-Blanket Water-Balloon Volleyball: Using beach

towels or blankets, toss water balloons back and forth over the net. A broken balloon on one side means a point for the opposition.

Then we divided into small groups for summer planning. Members discussed elements and activities they'd like to see in the summer program, and presented ideas to the whole group. We also had many good suggestions for alternate summer fun and ways to stay spiritually strong during the summer.

Luau-style snacks of fruit and cheese topped off our Summer Dreaming.

—Dave Pearce, Virginia Beach, Virginia

SWITCH HUNT

This crazy activity was a hit in our group. Here's how you can do it.

Advertise your Switch Hunt a couple of weeks ahead, but don't tell anyone what it is. Make sure you'll have enough drivers and vehicles to transport group members.

On the night of the event, get group members together and divide them into two teams. Give each team a pair of overalls, a clipboard and pencil, a tool chest, a different list of the same number of places to go (for example, stores,

private homes, the library, etc.), and a hat from your local utility company.

Explain: Your group must drive to each place. One person must put on the overalls and hat, carry the tool chest and clipboard and pencil and go up to the house (or whatever place you're at). He or she must tell the person/people that he or she is from the utility company (youth division), and they are doing a study called "Average Number of Light Switches." The group member must ask permission to go into the house along with some helpers and count the light switches. Once he or she gets the okay, the rest of the group members may go in to help. Keep a careful count of switches. Each new place you go, a new person must put on the overalls to make the introduction.

Tell the groups the time to meet back at the church and report how far they got.

When both groups are back, serve refreshments, let group members tell their stories, and award the winning group members light switch covers that have "Switch Hunt 1st Place" written on them.

—Scott Welch, Wilmore, Kentucky

THE BODY BEAUTIFUL

Here's a crowdbreaker to use before a study on 1 Corinthians 12.

Divide members into equal teams of no more than 10 per team. Object: First team to draw a complete body wins.

Provide newsprint, marking pens and a die for each team. Assign body parts to each number and post on newsprint:

1 = Head (eyes, ears, nose, mouth and hair)
2 = Trunk/chest
3 = One arm
4 = One hand
5 = One leg
6 = One foot

Place materials on a table at one end of the room. Have teams line up at the other end. One person from each team runs to the drawing table, rolls the die and draws the corresponding body part. The player returns to team members once the part is drawn and the game continues in relay fashion until all teams finish. (Note: If a body part is already drawn for the number rolled on the die, the player rolls until another part can be drawn. All body parts must connect.)

For added fun, show the "Bodies Beautiful" and have kids vote on the best, funniest, weirdest body.

—Gary K. Wheeler, Versailles, Kentucky

THE GREAT SLEIGH RACE

The next time it snows, get your group together at a great snow-sledding location and get ready for some fun!

Provide four sleds and divide group members into four teams, each with one rider and several pushers.

Give "maps" of the sledding route to the riders. The maps should give directions to the pit stops (for example, "Pass 12 trees on the left, turn right, pass barking dog,

turn left at the barn," etc.). Mark the pit stops with flags. When a team arrives at a pit stop, the rider refers to the map for instructions (for example, "All team members change coats"; "All run around the sled 10 times"; etc.).

If you have limited space but prefer a longer-lasting race, instruct teams to run through the course two or more times.

Let the winning team be the first to get its hot chocolate and cookies as everyone settles in a cozy room for a devotion on working together as a team for Christ.

—Burt Brock, Beckley, West Virginia

TOADS AND FROGS

Kids will leap to play this!

Pick a night when there's little wind and meet in a back yard or open field. Divide group members into two teams and give each team member a medium-sized candle. Label

28

one team "Toads" and the other "Frogs." Have teams go to opposite ends of the field and face each other.

Light candles and tell each team to exchange places and get to the other side of the playing field. The challenge? Team members must arrive at the other side with all their candles lighted. On the way to the other side it's okay to blow out the opponents' candles. If someone's candle is blown out (or goes out) that person must stop where he or she is and **not** attempt to blow out other candles. Stationary members must yell "toad" or "frog" (depending what team they're on); only team members can relight their teammates' extinguished flames.

The first team that makes it to the other side with all candles burning wins.

Here are more ideas:
- Play "You Light Up My Life" as background music.
- Hold an annual Toad-Frog Competition.
- Play "Leap Frog" to start.
- Have each team create a team song and sing it.
- Give a ceramic toadstool to the winning team.

So, what are you waiting for? Hop to it!

—Mark Eckel, Mandan, North Dakota

TOILET PAPER CONFESSIONS

This crazy crowdbreaker helps members get to know each other better.

Have your group sit in a circle and pass a roll of toilet paper from person to person. Instruct the young people to each take as much as they would need to blow their nose.

After everyone has taken some toilet paper, go around the circle and ask each person to tell one interesting fact about himself or herself for each square torn off.

This is great fun and everyone participates!

—Mary Albert, Richmond, Virginia

TOWEL SOCCER

This crazy soccer game will teach group members how to work together without getting all tangled up.

Begin by marking off a soccer field. (If you have a small group, you may want to use a smaller area.)

Divide group members into two even-numbered teams. Players then select someone from their team to be their partner, including goalies.

Each pair of team members is given a towel that they must hold by the corners throughout the entire game.

The soccer ball is thrown into play by the referee (a group leader or an extra group member). Partners must catch the ball in their towel and either pass it to another pair of kids on their team by flipping the ball up off the towel, or throwing it toward the goalies by flinging the ball from the towel.

Partners are allowed to take only three steps when they have the ball in their towel, then they must either pass it or try for a goal.

When the ball drops to the ground, the other team takes possession. Scoring is the same as regular soccer.

The fun is trying to avoid getting all tangled up with your partner as you try to make a goal for your team.

—Scott Welch, Athens, Georgia

VIDEO GAME FUN

If your group members enjoy video games, have a video game evening!

Meet at a group member's home, or take video game units, monitors (televisions), cartridges and controllers (paddles, joysticks, etc.) to your church. If many families can

30

loan these supplies, the church may be the better choice because you'd have more room.

Play team video: Group members pair off and sit back-to-back, with one partner facing the screen and the other partner holding the controller. Choose games such as Space Invaders; the partner who sees the screen calls out "left, right, fire," etc. Let pairs compete for the best score.

Do video relays: Divide your group into two equal teams and have each team line up behind a controller. Choose games such as PacMan and have players switch between rounds. The team with the highest score wins.

Remember to allow time for individual game playing and practicing. And don't forget the brief devotions and munchies to end the evening!

—Larry Walton, Roseburg, Oregon

WHO IS THE VISITOR?

Welcome youth group visitors by playing a game to guess each visitor's full name. Here's how it works.

Break your group into as many groups as there are letters in the visitor's name. For example, if Jo Nelson is the visitor, there should be eight small groups. Give each small group one letter from the name to act out without talking. Suggest pantomiming a biblical character, idea or event that begins with that same letter.

So, for Jo Nelson, group #1 might act out Jesus washing his disciples' feet. Once the whole group guesses the correct answer, "Jesus," everyone knows the visitor's first name starts with "J." Group #2 might act out a scene that portrays "obedience" to God, and group #3 might pose as the "Nativity" scene.

Jesus, obedience and Nativity correspond to the first three letters of Jo's name. Ask those who know the visitor's name not to tell.

This game is so enjoyable group members may actively recruit visitors.

—Mike Townsend, Elgin, Illinois

YUCK NIGHT

Many youth groups have different versions of Yuck Night. This is one plan for a gooey, yucky, warm-weather activity.

In your publicity, stress that kids wear old clothes. Select an outdoor site—or carefully cover the floor with plastic sheeting and newspaper.

Suggested activities:

1. Balloon toss—Fill balloons with tempera paint. Group members toss balloons to partners. Partners stand about six feet apart and move farther apart after each toss. When a balloon bursts, the partners drop out.

2. Apple bobbing—Use a large washtub and lots of apples with the stems still on them. No towels allowed.

3. Cracker grab—Immediately after the apple bob, do this game. With hands behind their backs, group members use only their teeth to pick up crackers buried in bowls of flour.

4. Papier-maché sculpting—Divide group members into teams of four to six. See which team can create the most interesting sculpture using strips of newspaper dipped into a flour-water paste. Save the sculptures for later, dry them and use them as piñatas for a future party.

5. Food feed—Divide group members into pairs. Blindfold one partner of each pair and have him or her keep hands behind the back. The other partner feeds him or her applesauce. Reverse roles.

6. Closing worship—Two possible scripture themes about cleansing are found in Acts 22:12-16 and Hebrews 10:19-22.

—Sylvia Carlson, Dallas, Texas

Group
Growth
Goodies

AMERICANS AND FOREIGNERS

For an interesting look at the American lifestyle we often take for granted, use this discussion starter.

Divide group members into small groups of four to six and choose one person from each group to be the American. Then have everyone else, the foreigners, give all of their purses, wallets, watches and jewelry to the American in their group.

Tell the Americans that they now own all of the possessions that belonged to the families of the foreigners. Tell the foreigners that all of them and their families now live together and must share all the possessions and food that were meant for only one family. Paint a picture that group members can relate to; tailor the tale of poverty to conditions in your own area.

Give group members time to think about and discuss what living like this would be like. Ask: "How does it feel to be rich/poor? How does it feel to know that others are rich/poor? Has this affected your relationship with God in any way?"

Use Matthew 25:31-46 for discussion afterward.

—Gloria Menke, Bolivar, Missouri

ANDREW CLUB

To increase youth group enthusiasm and attendance, form an Andrew Club. Andrew was always bringing people to Jesus—for example, Simon (John 1:40-42), the boy with the loaves and fish (John 6:8-9), the Greeks (John 12:20-22). A club in his honor would study about Andrew and challenge its members to "bring people to Jesus" too.

Have interested young people sign a sheet saying they will try to bring someone new to church (or Bible class or youth group) each month for a year, or a total of 12 times. Have occasional club meetings for members to study together and share successes and failures of being in the "Andrew Club."

Every year have a special service or meeting to award official Andrew Club members with Andrew Club T-shirts, jackets, plaques or certificates. This is also an opportunity to read notes of thanks from "visitors" who've become involved with the group because of "Andrew."

Along the same line, you could start a Barnabas Club. "Barnabas" means "one who encourages"; club members would be encouragers by remembering group members' birthdays with cards, cutting out and posting city or school newspaper articles highlighting group members, and regularly writing and sending notes of encouragement.

—Bryan Carter, Fort Collins, Colorado

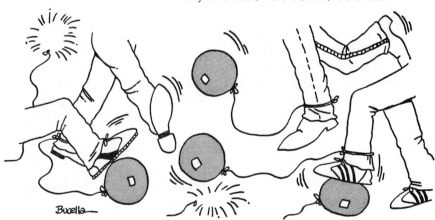

BALLOON PUTDOWNS

Decrease putdowns and increase compliments with the following activity.

Give a balloon and string to each young person as he or she enters the meeting room. Have the members blow up the balloons and tie them to their right ankles. Start the game: Instruct everyone to stomp on each other's balloons until they are all popped. Tell the young people to remember their feelings when their balloons are popped and when they pop others' balloons.

Then have members form small groups of three and discuss feelings. Ask: "How do you feel when your ego-balloon is popped at home? school? by your best friend? at youth group meeting?"

Form a circle and give each person a pencil and paper. Instruct each person to sign his or her name at the top of the page and pass it to the right. Pass the papers around the circle; ask the group members to write positive statements about each person on the appropriate paper. Continue until each person receives his or her paper back.

Compare the affirming statements to putdowns. Ask: "How do each of these types of statements make you feel? How does God want us to treat others? What are some ways to do that?"

Close by reading John 13:34. Pray for God's help as we build up others in the world.

—Frankie Garrick, Columbia, South Carolina

BOOKS FOR A SECRET FRIEND

This activity encourages unity in a group. It also works well in a retreat setting.

You'll need colored paper, pens, pencils, markers, crayons, magazines, scissors, staplers, glue, tape.

Gather group members together. Have everyone (including leaders) write his or her name on a piece of paper and place it in a basket. Everyone draws a name and becomes that person's secret friend for the duration of the event. Remind everyone to keep the name secret until the closing service.

Explain that each person is to make a booklet using pictures, drawings, poems, etc. The booklet reflects positive qualities such as talents, character and personality traits each person sees in his or her secret friend.

Show the booklets, reveal the secret friend's name and describe the booklet's contents one at a time during the closing prayer service. End with a group hug and familiar song.

—Mary Kay Fitzpatrick, St. Louis, Missouri

CHRISTMAS DEVOTION

Here's an activity to help your kids anticipate the Christmas season.

Ask your youth group members how they would complete the sentence, "Christmas is . . ." Give everyone a minute to write or think of a reply. At the count of three, have everyone simultaneously shout his or her sentence.

Explain: "That was difficult to understand, wasn't it? Sometimes the message of Christmas gets lost in the noise and celebration. We have to be quiet and listen to Jesus to get the real meaning of Christmas."

One at a time, ask each person to share how he or she completed the sentence, "Christmas is . . ."

Give each person an unlighted candle and have the group members sit in a circle in silence. Light the candles from one person to the next. When all candles are lighted, sing "Silent Night."

—Lee Hovel, York, Pennsylvania

CLIP-ART ALBUM

Getting tired of using "dog-eared" clip art every time you publicize a youth group activity? Or do you hate the hassle of using envelopes and file folders for clip art? Why not use a photo album for your clip-art collection?

Any photo album that allows for pages to be added to it will work. The clear plastic covering not only keeps your clip art clean and pressed flat, but also helps you find that special piece of artwork faster. Place tabs on the edges to mark special sections such as "Seasonal" (spring, summer, winter, fall), "Cartoons," "Bible," "Quips and Quotes" or "Camp."

A low-priced photo album sure makes each piece of artwork last a long time.

—Rick Chromey, Norfolk, Nebraska

CONTEMPORARY CHRISTIAN MUSIC RAFFLE

Every week I give away a cassette tape of a contemporary Christian group or singer I know will fit my young people's musical tastes. Here's how it works.

1. I buy a roll of tickets.

2. Each week, each person who attends a youth group meeting receives a ticket to write his or her name on, and turn in.

3. We sometimes play the tapes we have to give away as young people enter the meeting.

4. Someone draws a ticket and reads the name on the back. The winner gets to choose from several tapes.

5. If the person whose ticket was drawn isn't there, we draw another ticket.

6. Even though the tickets accumulate from week to week, I don't allow anyone to win twice until everyone has won once.

7. I also use the tickets as prizes for crowdbreaker winners.

When we travel somewhere together on a bus, I'm hearing more and more contemporary Christian music on their blasters.

—Dave Mahoney, Columbus, Indiana

DOLLAR BILL GIVEAWAY

You'd think anyone would take a no-strings-attached gift of money, but most people are suspicious or disinterested.

This activity helps your young people understand that sharing their faith can be as difficult as giving money away.

Divide your group into pairs (threes at the most) and take

them to a shopping mall. Give each pair one brand-new dollar bill.

The goal is to give the new dollar away. The kids must not offer any explanation or even say they are part of a church group. They must simply give the dollar to a stranger.

Only three places are off-limits: video game rooms, restrooms and Christian bookstores. Set a time limit and designate a meeting place.

Have at least one adult stay at the meeting place during the exercise to help with any problems. That adult might have a second dollar bill for teams who manage to give their first dollar away.

You might also want to plan an activity for those who finish early. For instance, make advance arrangements with a Christian bookstore to let the kids listen to Christian music when they finish. Promise the manager careful supervision of the group.

Return to the church for debriefing and worship. Discuss how it feels to be rejected. Help your kids relate this activity to sharing their Christian faith with others and the fear that goes with witnessing. Remind your group that some people readily accept witnessing, some are suspicious, some are angry, some are puzzled.

Close with a time of worship using Christian witness as your theme. This activity can help prepare your group for a mission trip or week.

—Bill Davis, Kansas City, Kansas

39

DOUBLE-DUTY GIVING

No doubt you've heard of gift certificates. But did you ever think of sending Promise for Improved Conduct certificates as Christmas greetings? Challenge your group members to give these!

Have your young people fold sheets of construction paper to resemble Christmas cards and paste on Christmas seals or pictures. Have them print in large letters across the top: Promise for Improved Conduct. The parents will be so shocked when they read those words that they won't be able to wait to look inside.

The message inside might read like this: "Mom, I'm sorry I do so many things that annoy you. This Christmas I want to put the 'peace on earth' theme to work. I'm going to listen to you more closely, choose my words more carefully and do my part to keep up with the chores. When I fail, I hope you'll pray for me and know that I'm trying my best."

Take any other situation that bothers your young people and adapt the Promise for Improved Conduct to the individual circumstance. If a young person has a problem in school, this is a good way for him or her to show the teacher that he or she wants to change. Your young people can also use the certificates for Sunday school teachers and pastors to let them know that they've heard what they are teaching.

By taking such a bold step toward self-improvement, young people can show they mean business.

Encourage your group members to follow through with

this type of giving; remind them that they'll be in for a surprise. What fun to find a gift that serves double duty. First, they make someone happy, then they get happy themselves through the joy of giving and the satisfaction of making progress toward a goal.

—Esther M. Bailey, Phoenix, Arizona

FAME

Here's an activity sure to generate discussion on fame and the definition of real "importance."

Begin by providing newsprint, colored construction paper, ribbons, markers, tape, etc. and instructing group members to create a "fame costume" for one member of the group.

When they've finished making one member "famous," ask group members to discuss the significance of the costume. Why did they decorate the "famous" member of the group as they did?

Ask: "Who are some famous people you've met? Who are some famous people you'd like to get to know? Why?

What qualities do you think they have that you want?"

Put pictures of 10 famous people on the wall and ask group members to rank them in order of most to least famous. Have members list on newsprint or on the "fame costume" the elements of fame they used to make their decisions.

Add another picture: one of Jesus. Put it right up there, next to the president. Discuss ways in which elements of fame fit Jesus. Ask: "How would the media treat Jesus today? Would he be famous? Why or why not?"

Mention that although Jesus may not be a famous person from the world's point of view, he is the greatest person we can ever meet. Close with a brief discussion on God's view of importance.

—Phil Print, Denver, Colorado

FEBRUARY LOVE-IN

Here's a way for your young people to show love.

Hold a group meeting at the beginning of February. Have each member choose a scripture passage about love and write it down.

Explain the meeting's purpose: to make a paper chain of love and present it to the congregation.

Have members each write on strips of newsprint their love scripture references. Have kids write Bible references only—not the passages.

Supply Bible concordances so kids can find the exact references if they don't know them by heart. Then let half the kids look up more verses on love and the other half write them down on newsprint strips. Play songs about love while kids work. Play games during breaks and serve refreshments.

Tape the strips of newsprint together to form a long

chain. Carefully store the chain till the Sunday before Valentine's Day. Then present the chain to your congregation by circling everyone with it; bring together the chain's two ends at the front of the church. As the families leave for home ask them to tear off a scripture verse, look it up, and read it with family members.

—Linda Owens, Hicksville, Ohio

GOLDEN LIPS AWARD

If the kids in your youth group are interruptive or talk when they're not supposed to during meetings, try this idea.

Cut a large pair of lips out of yellow posterboard. Print in bold letters across the lips: Golden Lips Award. Each week give this traveling award to the person who's the most quiet during the meeting. Have that person bring back the award the following week and give it to someone else. It's a good idea to have two or three copies of the lips in case someone forgets to bring them back.

Other lip awards could be given also, such as a Pink Lips Award for the person who smiles the most during the meeting, or a White Lips Award for the "good guy" person who says kind things to other group members.

—Jane Erickson, Covington, Tennessee

GROUP GREETING CARDS

This simple idea promotes group spirit and a sense of caring among members. You'll need 11 large sheets of paper or posterboard, and bright-colored markers.

Print one letter of the phrase "Get Well Soon" on each sheet. Have group members huddle together holding the letters, and photograph the group. Have many prints made.

When a group member or friend is ill, have everyone sign a get-well card, and send it along with the group photo.

Also use this idea to send other messages: "Happy Birthday"; "Have a Fun Trip"; or "We Miss You" to a member who hasn't attended group meetings for a while. The possibilities are endless.

—Jeff Graham, Fisher, Illinois

KICK-OFF DINNER

Last September our group welcomed the fall with a Kick-Off Dinner. You can do the same this year.

Send group members invitations saying, "You're invited to a Kick-Off Dinner!" List the date, time, place, and encourage them to "Come and have a ball!"

We had spaghetti and meatballs for dinner. Then a short presentation outlined plans to "have a ball" during the year in youth group.

We played (what else?) ball games, including relays with balls. Our favorite relay uses paper bags (one for each team) filled identically with various kinds of balls: cotton balls, sourballs, pingpong balls, gum balls, baseballs, footballs, balls of socks, and even ball point pens! Place the bags on a table and attach to each bag a list of the items enclosed. Each team member runs up, in turn, reads aloud the ball he or she is to find (following the order on the list), then reaches in without looking, pulls out the correct item for all to see, places it back in the bag and returns to his or her team. The first team to get through all the items (or team members, whichever is more) wins.

Award members of winning teams with gum balls, ball point pens, etc. And give other ball-related items for prizes throughout the evening.

—Linda Feree, Pittsburgh, Pennsylvania

LOVE LINE

Use letter-writing to build closer, more meaningful relationships.

You need a clothesline and clothespins. Give group members each a clothespin and have them write their name on it. String the line where it's easily accessible, and place the clothespins on it.

Have the group members write to each other notes of love, appreciation and/or encouragement. Stress that the notes should be positive; no putdowns allowed. Group members may write the notes on a special night or over a long period of time. Clip notes to individuals' pins. Writers may include their names or leave notes unsigned.

Make sure everyone receives notes; recruit members to write to those who receive few.

Your whole group will discover the thrill of spreading and receiving words of love and thanks.

—Will Horton, Bethany, Oklahoma

NERD NIGHT

That's right, Nerd Night. Believe it or not, this bizarre evening can be a powerful object lesson.

When promoting Nerd Night, require group members to dress as nerds (white socks, short pants, thick glasses, etc.). Announce that those judged to be the three best-dressed nerds will win prizes.

The night of the party, have extra nerd clothing on hand

for those who come unprepared. Play special nerd games you create; develop rules for games such as "Name That Nerd" or "Hand-Held Calculator Races" or "Lifestyles of the Dull."

After the games, have judges announce the three best-dressed nerds and ask that prizes be given to them. The group leader then admits he or she forgot to buy prizes.

Sponsors announce that the only solution is for everyone to go to a nearby shopping center. Of course, the "nerds" will be hesitant to be seen in public dressed as they are. Convince them that there is strength in numbers, and head for the mall. Even though the teenagers will want to rush through the mall, take your time.

After the shopping spree, return to the church to discuss how group members felt (and to give out prizes). Center devotions on how God made people different, but all God's children have feelings and the need to be accepted. Use Matthew 23:11-12; Luke 5:27-32; John 8:2-11; or Philippians 4:8-9.

—Rex Brown, Fort Mitchell, Kentucky

PHONE DEVOTIONS

Do your young people have trouble with their daily devotions? Do they spend too much time on the phone? Consider this.

We've set up a daily youth devotional phone line. A young person can call and listen to an upbeat, 2½-minute devotion. There is a new message every day on the church's two phone answering machines. In addition, a phone number where I can be reached is given for those who want to talk with someone.

We promoted this by blitzing our local schools and concerts with sharp-looking business-size cards which display the phone number and theme, "A dynamite call for a lift." We found that many "outside" kids who won't come to a church will call for the message. A particular series on suicide, for example, resulted in many kids calling for help and finding it.

There has been an additional impact on our youth group members too. On weekends they take turns telling about their faith life or giving a brief devotion on the tape. Then they tell their friends to call, and thus become more bold in their Christian witness.

Finally, at the end of the message I briefly give the details of our upcoming events.

It takes some work to pull this off well, but I have found it to be more than worth the effort!

—Steven French, Wheaton, Illinois

PHOTO POST CARDS

You ought to be in pictures—particularly on the back of post cards.

This idea helps build group membership and is fun and easy to do.

47

Gather your youth group in front of your church for a group photograph. Have the kids "ham it up" for the camera by looking "friendly." Have them wave, smile, cheer, jump up and down, laugh or give thumbs up.

Use black-and-white film so the pictures will easily reproduce on an offset press. Use a 35mm camera, if possible, so the photos will be post-card size.

Add a greeting and/or the name of your youth group or church across the bottom of the photo with press-on letters from a local art store.

Mail post cards to kids in your group for any reason you can think of Kids like seeing themselves on the cards. Plus, they can see what an important part of your group they really are.

—David Gottshall, San Angelo, Texas

PRAISING STONES

Here's a vivid illustration of Luke 19:37-40.

Collect tempera paint, brushes, water, bits of felt, scissors, yarn, glue and cotton balls. Give each person a smooth stone (about one or two inches in diameter).

Have kids sit in a circle; place the craft materials in the center. Instruct group members to paint faces on their stones using the felt and cotton balls for hair. Then read Luke 19:37-40.

Say that no one has actually heard rocks praise God but they're capable of doing it if humans won't. Tell everyone to praise God rather than have the "stones" do it.

For added fun, pass around toothpicks with small squares of paper. Have kids create scripture signs and attach them to their stones with glue or tape. Or vote on the ugliest or prettiest stone. Announce the winner as "The Best Rock of Ages."

—Mark Lundborg, Silver Springs, Florida

PRAYER PARTNERS

Our church has found an exciting way to involve adults in the youth ministry and help the teenagers feel really special. We call it the Prayer Partner program.

Recruit adults of all ages who are willing to commit themselves to pray for a teenager for one year. Assign each adult a young person to pray for and provide basic information about him or her (name, address, age and birthday, hobbies and interests, church involvement, etc.). Encourage the adults to send notes and birthday cards, and recognize special achievements.

Keep Prayer Partners secret throughout the year. You will need one person, though, to relay information between the Prayer Partners and the young people. The teenagers may want to correspond with their Prayer Partners about prayer needs or appreciation for cards, notes, etc.

Between Christmas and New Year's Day, we hold an evening reception where young people and Prayer Partners meet. It's always a beautiful time when the teenagers learn who their adult pray-ers have been.

—David A. Ashworth, Cincinnati, Ohio

PROGRESSIVE PUBLICITY

How do you publicize an event or activity so that everyone becomes interested?

This idea worked for me in my effort to publicize a study

of the Old and New Testament, titled "Something Old, Something New."

One month in advance, I placed the letters "SOSN" on small pieces of paper around the church. The next week I added the date of the Bible study. Then the next week I placed the time, place, etc., until eventually all the information was added.

Everyone had fun figuring out what the letters "SOSN" stood for and trying to guess the upcoming activity.

As a result of this publicity, all group members were interested and the Bible study was well-attended.

—Jeff Swedenburg, Louisville, Kentucky

PUMPKIN SYMBOLS

What activity could be more "cut out" for Halloween than pumpkin carving?

Add a creative idea to a youth group pumpkin-carving party: Slice Christian words or symbols instead of faces in the pumpkins.

You'll need sharp knives, old newspapers, candles, plenty of pumpkins and lots of enthusiastic carvers!

Ask each person to carve a Christian word or symbol that's especially meaningful to him or her.

End the evening with a candlelight worship service in the church. Place candles inside the pumpkins and arrange your carved works of art throughout the sanctuary. Display pumpkins on the pulpit, altar, floor—wherever. The soft, orange glow shining through the words creates a special worshipful atmosphere.

If you want to speak of God's spirit shining through each person, use Galatians 5:22-23. For a reminder that each person is the light of the world, refer to Matthew 5:14-16. Or if you want to emphasize Jesus as the light, read John 1:1-14.

For a seedy snack—wash, salt and roast the pumpkin seeds in a low-temperature oven. Serve them for an after-carving snack!

Encourage young people to take their masterpieces home. Suggest displaying them in their windows as a shining Christian witness!

—Trinity Lutheran Church, Hudson, Wisconsin

REASONS OR EXCUSES?

Try this to ignite a discussion on church attendance. Ask each group member to write five good reasons for attending church. Have members compare, discuss and then rank the reasons from "best" to "worst."

Next ask each group member to write five good reasons for **not** attending church. Encourage them to list ones they've used, they hope to use, they know friends use, and others they think are worth mentioning. Then again compare, discuss and rank the reasons.

My group members did this and when we discussed the reasons in light of Hebrews 10:25 we discovered that some of the reasons gradually became excuses.

But what a discussion!

—Rick Allen, Uvalde, Texas

SANTA'S SECRET SERVICE

Not the night before Christmas, but 10 nights before, begin this activity.

Have your group members pretend they belong to

Santa's Secret Service and choose one or more special families to surprise. The special family might be well-liked, motherless or fatherless, new to the neighborhood or have a handicapped member.

Each of the 10 nights before Christmas, Santa's Secret Service leaves a small wrapped gift at the special family's front door. (Gifts can include cookies, jam, holly, a huge homemade Christmas card, a gift certificate, Christmas napkins, a red candle, etc.)

Leave the gifts at different times each evening, ring the doorbell and run!

The special family will ask everyone, "Who's leaving these gifts at our door?" But Santa's Secret Service members keep their secret and gleefully plan their next surprise!

—Janet Balmforth, Provo, Utah

SELF-IMAGE OBJECTS

This activity helps your group members learn more about each other and themselves as well.

Ask the young people each to bring three objects to the next youth group meeting. One object represents how they think others see them; one shows how they see themselves; one shows how they would like others to see them. The objects may be either abstract or concrete. For instance, objects may be poems, pictures, quotations, books, or keepsakes.

At the meeting, have each person show his or her objects and explain why he or she chose those particular items.

—Daniel G. Felts, Bridgeton, Missouri

SIGNED, ANONYMOUS

The U.S. Postal Service can be your ally in creating interest in activities at your church. Approximately five weeks before a special youth group event, send cards to teenagers who are associated with your church but don't normally attend youth functions. Let's say the event is the showing of a film titled **The Question** on May 15 at the church. The cards will simply say "May 15" and not be signed.

The next three weeks, do the same; send unsigned cards with the date. Use a different type of card for each mailing. Change-of-address post cards from the post office or cards from local motels will do fine.

The week before the event, use official church letterhead or post cards to send a signed message that reads something like this:

May 15: Sound familiar?

May 15: Film, **The Question**

May 15: The Fireside Room at (church's name and address)

May 15: Be there

This approach adds to the church's postage expense, but also adds interest among kids. And that's worth the investment.

—Sam Crabtree, Brookings, South Dakota

SOFA STUFF

This idea put our old sofa in the youth room to use and

encouraged better youth attendance for the Wednesday evening meetings.

During a meeting, have all of your young people pile on the sofa. Take a photo of the group, preferably with an instant-print camera. Hang the photo over the sofa and include the date and total number of kids who were present.

Your group members will soon be talking about breaking the Sofa Stuff record.

Within three weeks of the start of our Sofa Stuff photos, we doubled our average attendance.

—Bill Davis, Kansas City, Missouri

SWAP LABOR FOR FUN

Ever wish you could take your group on a cruise or stay at an expensive resort? Here's a way you can make it happen. All it takes is a little research and a lot of sweat.

First, find a charter cruise service, state-owned resort or riding stable in your area.

Next, look for a project at the site requiring unskilled labor. For example, we presented the owner of a yacht charter service with a written offer to clean off the beach and paint fences for the beginning of the season. Our offer included who would furnish materials and tools, when the work would be done and what services our group would receive in return.

The owner was so pleased when we finished that he immediately invited us to return the next year. He also hired two members of our group as regular help for the season! And, several more kids used this idea to find their own summer jobs.

This fun project brought our group closer together and made an out-of-reach activity affordable.

—Bill Hubbard, Bigfork, Montana

TALENT MATCH

Use this game to start off a program on self-esteem. Show your group members that some talents are deeper than visible characteristics.

Send three or more people out of the room. Give everyone else a piece of paper and a marker. Ask the group members to write one thing they do well (e.g., sing, babysit, study, get along with parents). Collect the papers.

One at a time, invite the other group members back into the room and give each 30 seconds (depending on the number of young people) to place the "talent papers" in front of the correct owners. Those correctly matched stand up, and the guesser keeps changing the rest of the papers until the time is up. The person with the greatest number of matches wins.

Talk about the abilities and talents we might overlook, but other people notice. Read Matthew 25:14-30 and discuss how we should use all of our talents and abilities.

—Scott Welch, Wilmore, Kentucky

THE ENVELOPE PLEASE!

This communication technique can have as many forms as you have ideas. Use it to add a touch of mystery and an atmosphere of involvement. Here's how it works.

When you plan a talk or presentation, plan spots where illustration would be helpful. Before your presentation, hand out specially prepared and numbered envelopes, boxes, paper sacks, etc., to group members.

Then during the presentation, call out the numbers when you're ready for them. Depending on the nature of your talk, have in the containers: symbolic objects or pictures; instructions (to read, draw, act out or sing something); a cassette tape to play; a problem to solve (such as how the

group can share one stick of gum—provided); treats for everyone (such as candies, balloons, etc.); or whatever else would be appropriate to your presentation.

For example, at one point in a talk, I asked the question "How do we get to heaven?" After a brief discussion, I called out an envelope number. A girl opened it and revealed the mystery object: a key that had "Jesus" inscribed on it.

—Karen Darling, Kelseyville, California

TRIP TALK

Transform those long, tiresome bus trips into productive group-building experiences. Here are several ideas to help your young people get to know each other better.

Begin by challenging each member to get to know everyone else on the bus by the end of the journey. Then have the kids arrange themselves alphabetically (by last names) two to a seat. Tell members to learn three new facts about their seat partner in addition to the person's name, and have each person introduce his or her partner to the whole bus.

Next, form groups of four by having designated pairs turn around and face another pair without changing seats. Each person in the foursome tells what he or she did the past weekend. Allow time for the four friends to visit.

Try having the whole group rearrange themselves by their birthdays, still two to a seat. Again form groups of four, and have each person complete the sentence: "The best birthday party I ever had was . . ." After allowing enough time for more visiting, have them complete: "The best birthday present I ever received was . . ." Give kids time to visit before rearranging the group again.

Continue this process throughout your trip. Before the trip, have a committee of kids help think of other seating arrangement possibilities (for instance: shoe size, favorite color, hair color). Dream up sentence completion possibilities that will stimulate conversation, break down barriers and create new friendships.

—Terry Caouette, Duluth, Minnesota

TWO GREATEST COMMANDMENTS

Use this service to emphasize the two greatest commandments.

Above the meeting room door, hang a banner that says "Love the Lord your God with all your heart." Above the sanctuary entrance, hang a banner that says "Love your neighbor as yourself." For each group member, fill two communion cups: one with pure water and the other with water and a pinch of salt. Leave these filled cups in the meeting room.

Before the young people enter the meeting room, ask them to wear choir robes and remove their shoes. Say that they are about to enter the Holy of Holies and there is to be no talking or laughing. Inside the room, light a candle and have each person drink a communion cup filled with water, which represents God's purity. Then have each drink the cup of salt water, which represents our impurity. The message: Even small sins are noticeable to God, yet he commands us to love him with all our heart. He wants our love. Close this portion by saying a liturgical prayer.

Give each young person a lighted candle to carry into the sanctuary. Once inside, sing songs of praise to Jesus for his Resurrection. Discuss how much Jesus loves us and how much we should love others. Ask: "What are some ways we can 'love our neighbor as ourself'?"

Your youth group will always remember this service **and** the two greatest commandments.

—Jon Adams, Crosby, Minnesota

UNEMPLOYMENT LINE

Generate discussion on vocations with this game.

Before your group meets, place a box in the center of the meeting room. On separate pieces of paper write 50 occupations (for example, teacher, lawyer, trash collector, dog catcher, circus clown, etc.). Fold these and put them in the box.

When group members arrive, form four teams and place each in a corner of the room. Explain: "On the word 'go,' one person from each team runs to the box and picks a piece of paper. He or she runs back to the team and pantomimes the vocation until the team guesses it. The game continues until each person has a chance to pantomime a job. First team done wins."

Read Colossians 3:12-17 and discuss the qualities God wants to establish in us—on the job or off.

—Scott Welch, Wilmore, Kentucky

Fun
Fund
Raisers

BUSINESS CAR WASH

A new twist in car washes: Plan a car wash to service business people and companies.

Set your date for a Friday (during a school vacation or day off) and choose an available parking lot in the central part of the city. Earlier in the week, visit businesses and make appointments to pick up employee and company cars during office hours to wash and clean the autos. (Check your church insurance policy to see if it covers damage to cars.)

Also check the Yellow Pages for locations of any industri- al parks or companies that would have lots of company cars (for example, cab companies or truck and bus firms).

We found that working people appreciate this conven- ience; they don't have to spend weekend time getting their cars washed.

Our fee when we do this is donations only, but we aver- age $5 a car and earn more than $300 a day, with 15 to 20 group members picking up, washing, cleaning and return- ing the vehicles.

If possible, plan this once a month and build your clientele.

—Terry Walthall, Springfield, Missouri

CALVARY COOKIE FACTORY

We capitalized on people's basic love of home-baked chocolate chip cookies and made a fortune.

You can too, especially if your church is near a college or university.

Our church is several blocks from the U.S. Naval Academy stadium. Last football season we began selling freshly baked chocolate chip cookies after each of the four home football games.

The project was so successful and the cookies so popular that we began to look for a way to continue the project after the football season ended. We decided to open a "Care Package Service."

We sent letters and order forms to 21 parents clubs around the country (addresses provided by the Academy) and explained our program, offering to deliver cookies to their sons and daughters on four dates selected to correspond with exam periods at the Academy (in January, February, March and April). The order forms allowed room for a message to the receiver of the cookies.

The orders piled in, with checks for $1.50 per dozen cookies. We organized for action: We needed bakers, wrappers, bag logo designers and artists, gift tag writers, and deliverers. Ten to 12 young people were involved in each production, scheduled on Friday evenings and Saturday mornings.

In January and February, we baked and delivered about 175 dozen cookies. By March, as news of the service continued to spread, orders totaled nearly 250 dozen, with numerous notes of appreciation from parents and requests to continue our project in the fall.

Total receipts from the eight sales (four football games and four exam periods) amounted to nearly $2,000. After expenses for ingredients and supplies, we netted $1,000.
—Beverly Henry, Annapolis, Maryland

COMEDY VIDEOS

The young people in the youth group and I combined our love for media with the group's creative flair and came up with a delightful and effective fund raiser. Comedy Videos gives us a chance to have fun on film.

Here's how to develop your own comedy video fund raiser:

First, have a place in your church where people can sign up to have a video made. A small table in the foyer is ideal.

Have interested people complete an Information Form, leave a blank video cassette and $5.

The Information Form includes a description of the basic plot and setting. For instance, someone's anniversary, birthday party, first date, etc. Have a place to list the characters in the movie, their age and personality type (they're shy; funny; always serious) and then any instructions as far as what sort of conversation took place or order of events. (On some of the Information Forms, people left it up to our own imagination to create funny situations.) An Information Form looks like this:

Video Information Form

Fill in this form as completely as possible. We'll make up any information you don't provide.

Persons you want in the movie:

Name	Age	Personality Type
1.		
2.		
3.		
4.		
5.		

Briefly describe the basic plot and setting you'd like to see in your movie:

Any special instructions, situations or scenes you'd like to see in this movie?

Take the Information Form and make a 10 to 15 minute movie. Set up a special room in your church as the production studio complete with props and backdrops.

One family in our church listed their cross-country summer vacation—every place they visited, what they did and who they saw. The main characters were a mom, dad and three daughters. One place they visited was the Grand Canyon.

When the time came to produce the comedy video, three guys dressed up as little girls. In the opening scene we went outside. The father loaded suitcases onto the roof of a car and they kept falling off and opening up. We used a washtub with rocks in it for the Grand Canyon and had our character family look down into the tub. We tried just about anything and everything we could think of to make it funny.

After you've made a number of videos, set a date for a special showing for the whole congregation. You might want to plan a banquet and charge admission. For additional fun, have people guess which family is being portrayed in each video.

Although the fund raiser is over, we already have started a waiting list for the next comedy video season.

—Scott Welch, North East, Maryland

EASTER BASKET FACTORY

Want a new fund raiser? Have your group create and sell Easter baskets.

For traditional baskets, ask each youth group member to donate a different type of candy (for example, jelly beans, malted-milk balls, marshmallow eggs, chocolate bunnies). For health-food Easter baskets, have the young people donate hard-boiled eggs, bananas, oranges, raisins. Instead of chocolate bunnies, create fruit bunnies: Use two bananas for ears, an orange for the head and use toothpicks to attach raisins for the eyes and nose.

Also include in the Easter baskets, tokens of Easter such as miniature crosses, butterfly or rainbow stickers, packets of flower seeds, rolled-up scrolls of Easter Bible verses inside colored plastic eggs, balloons.

Baskets, ribbons and decorative grass are inexpensive and can be purchased at discount stores.

Gather the group members one afternoon and form an Easter basket assembly line. Wrap the filled baskets with clear plastic wrap, tied securely with a bow. Price the different-sized baskets; then begin selling!

We profit at least 50 percent each year we sell the baskets. We even have people order the baskets ahead for the next year!

—Keith Stagge, Milford, Ohio

FOUR SQUARE TOURNEY

The next time you get together with several churches in your area, try this mixer—Four Square Tourney. This activity equalizes groups of different sizes and individuals of varied athletic ability. It encourages making new friends too.

The rules of this game vary a bit, but basically they are as follows: A 16-foot-by-16-foot square is drawn on the floor and divided into quarters. The quarters are numbered one through four. A player stands in each square; extra players line up by the fourth square.

The player in the first square starts by bouncing the ball in his or her square and hitting it underhand to another square. The receiver hits the ball into another square. A player is "out" if he or she hits the ball out of the 16-foot square, lets the ball bounce more than once in his or her square, steps in someone else's square or holds the ball.

When a person is "out" he or she goes to the end of the line and another person rotates in.

Find referees who will also act as scorekeepers for each 10 to 15 persons. With masking tape, mark off squares according to the rules on any suitable surface. You need enough playground balls and a good ball pump just in case.

Here's how the tournament works:
● Everyone attending participates.
● Group members are assigned to squares randomly.

They will play **for** their group but not necessarily **with** their group.

● Give points after the first serve in each square. After play begins, a point for each group counts each time a member of that group serves.

● When time is called, all play stops. Referees add scores for each group and divide by the number of players in that group. The highest average score wins.

Use this activity as a fund raiser by charging a small entry fee. Round out the event with refreshments and a worship service.

—First United Methodist Church, Denton, Texas

HUGS FOR H.O.P.E

How often have you seen the bumper sticker that says, ''Have you hugged your kid today?'' Kids aren't the only ones who deserve a hug every day. This fund raiser allows worshipers to receive hugs from youth group members in exchange for contributions. Everyone seems to love the idea.

Announce your fund-raising idea near Valentine's Day or when your pastor preaches a sermon on love, hunger or missions. Actually, any Sunday is appropriate. You might want to earmark proceeds for a special fund to help the needy of your church or community. You could call this special fund H.O.P.E.: Help Our People in Emergency.

After setting a date for your fund raiser, here's all you do: Buy posterboard and marking pens. Have kids draw up announcements emphasizing what H.O.P.E. is and how you'll use the proceeds. Hang the posters around the church. Encourage each ''hugger'' to make his or her own contribution box.

You may want to make ''hug coupons'' that people purchase and keep to get hugs throughout the year. These coupons entitle the owner to a hug from any youth group member. Make hug coupons from 3x5 index cards using the following words: **The bearer of this coupon is entitled to one hug from any youth group member at any time throughout the year.** You may want to draw a heart with the words, ''Hugs for H.O.P.E.'' printed on it. You could also write scriptures about love on the cards.

Announce the fund raiser during worship and set a time limit for the hugging. Have the kids go around to members of the congregation soliciting hugs and selling hug coupons.

Hugs for H.O.P.E. is a great self-esteem builder for everyone. Besides, everyone benefits from a hug.

—James Yoder Jr., Annville, Pennsylvania

HUNGER SCAVENGER HUNT

Instead of the usual "Let's collect canned goods for the poor," we added a new twist. Here's how you can too.

Call a local food distribution center and explain the project. Set a day three weeks away for your group to deliver the collected food.

Announce the beginning of the Hunger Scavenger Hunt (have some enthusiastic group members help) and hand out the list of items to be found. The list should also include the number of points per pound, can, box, dollar, etc. that will be awarded.

Pair off group members and challenge them to contact stores, neighbors and church members. They should explain what they're doing and ask for vitamins, canned goods, money, frozen turkeys, ham or other meats.

On the designated day, have the pairs bring their collected food items to the church. Tally the points for every pound, can or dollar collected. We gave a surprise gift—a frozen chicken—to the pair with the most points. They donated it to the hunger project!

Gather the items in a truck and deliver them to the center.

All of our young people had fun and want to do this project again.

—Karl Whiteman, Grandville, Michigan

Item	Points
Powdered milk	1 pt. per lb.
Turkey (whole, frozen)	5 pts. per lb.
Ham (canned)	4 pts. per lb.
Rice	2 pts. per lb.
Beans (dry)	2 pts. per lb.
Sugar	2 pts. per lb.
Flour	2 pts. per lb.
Macaroni or spaghetti	1 pt. per lb.
Noodles	1 pt. per lb.
Canned vegetables	1 pt. per can
Peanut butter	4 pts. per jar
Cake/cookie/brownie mix	2 pts. per box
Canned fruit	1 pt. per can
Vitamins (multi-type)	3 pts. per 100
Soup (cans or mixes)	2 pts. each
Cooking oil	3 pts. per bottle
Shortening (Crisco type)	3 pts. per can
Canned meat (tuna, corned beef, etc.)	3 pts. per can
Jello/pudding (cans or boxes)	1 pt. each
$ Money $ (to purchase food)	1 pt. per $1.00
(Other items will be judged accordingly)	

LUNCHES TO GO

Most people plan to do something after church or are hungry immediately following the service. Making Sunday lunch a convenience is a temptation hardly anyone can refuse. Our fund raiser offers Sunday Lunches to Go. Brown paper bags and simple foods make this activity easy and fun as well as a positive service to the people in your congregation.

Start by choosing simple lunch items: sandwiches, fruit, milk or juice, brownies or cookies, napkins and plastic silverware. You may also want to include a surprise snack such as scripture cards taped to a Hershey's Kiss. You might want to have kids write scripture passages on pieces of paper to insert with the lunch. Using markers, decorate the lunch sacks with designs. Advertise them as "designer lunches." Set up a table in the foyer. Drape it in a tablecloth and decorate with crepe paper. Have signs that say: "Lunches to Go." Ask teenage servers to wear aprons or chefs' hats.

Prepare the lunches before the church service. Don't set a price for the lunches but allow people to offer donations. Have someone give an announcement in the morning service about the Lunches to Go fund raiser. Take photos during the fund raiser. Make a poster a week after the event with the pictures and total amount raised. Put it up on a church bulletin board.

Use this idea once a year; perhaps more often. Summer is an excellent time of the year for Lunches to Go, when people are involved in outdoor activities and may not have enough time to fix their own lunch.

—Phyllis Hill, Springfield, Ohio

MAKE MONEY WITH MANUFACTURERS' REFUNDS

Here's an idea to help finance your group's next project.

Manufacturers pay money for the proof of purchases on specified products. Save boxes, labels, containers, lids and receipts.

Then make an orderly refunding bank. Use these two categories: Food—edible items; Non-food—non-edible items. Use a large box, envelope or plastic bag for files.

Obtain refund forms from grocery stores, drug stores, auto centers. These forms are small printed pieces of paper that say something such as, "$1.00 back for four UPCs from our product." (UPCs or Universal Pricing Codes are the bars and numbers on products signaling their prices.)

Check store bulletin boards and aisles each week for refund forms. Most stores don't limit the number of forms you take, but only take as many as you can use.

Gather forms and file them in a small box according to their expiration dates.

Each person takes one of the different forms and collects the correct number of items from the refunding bank. Each member fills out the form with his or her own name, home address, and then mails it. Most offers limit one per person, address or household so read the fine print.

Have fun raising money.

—Peggy Adams, Oklahoma City, Oklahoma

PARENTS DAY OFF

Our youth group renewed funds with this old idea: sitting for children on a Saturday.

First we planned our strategy: games, coloring and craft projects, bike riding, soccer, softball, etc., all based at the church. Soup and sandwiches are the perfect lunch (especially with lots of peanut butter and jelly).

Then we publicized our services and fees: one child, all day (9 to 5), lunch included, $7; one child, half day (9 to 1), lunch included, $4; two or three children, all day, lunch included, $10; two or three children, half day, lunch included, $6; four or five children, all day, lunch included,

$12; four or five children, half day, lunch included, $8.

Parents dropped off their kids at 9 a.m. and paid when they picked them up. They love this service! One parent reported being grateful for the chance to clean the house—all at once! Others went on day trips, visited special friends, or just spent some time alone.

Note: While this fund raiser is always **timely** (ask any parent), some **times** may be more productive for your youth fund: for example, Christmas shopping season, Mother's and Father's Day weekends, etc. Or—you might consider providing this service once a month!

—Charyla Olsen, Hemet, California

PERSONALIZED PUPPET SHOWS

This simple idea has taken us a long way.

Our puppet group, the Youth Puppeteers, has presented numerous programs in various settings. At one of our meetings, a group member suggested we "personalize" the presentations. She explained: "Let's find out names of people in the organizations where we perform and some information about them. Then we can make up our own skits with stories about these people and some of the humorous things that have happened to them."

The course of our Youth Puppeteers changed. It became important to know our schedule six weeks to two months in advance. With new enthusiasm, young people question the persons who invite us to do programs and get needed information: names of some people who will be present, some things they're known for (or kidded about), and any general facts about the group itself.

With that information, we now tailor our programs to each special audience. The Youth Puppeteers feel an increased sense of enjoyment and ministry as they carefully prepare for each audience.

Skits are written and special recordings made for each program. But this work is more "fun" for the 26 members involved.

We first presented a personalized program at the graduation banquet of our Community Hospital School of Nursing.

Our expenses are mainly the time and talent of the young people, since we already have our puppets and stage. In two years we have earned over $450 in contributions for doing our Personalized Puppet Shows.

—Dr. George K. Bowers, Roanoke, Virginia

PHOTOGRAPHING PETS FOR PROFIT

For fun and funds, your youth group can run a pet portrait service! Many people consider pets "part of the family," but few portrait studios photograph pets.

Advertise your service in church newsletters, school newspapers, and on community bulletin boards. Once you get started, word of mouth will keep customers coming to you.

Use a 35mm single-lens reflex camera. Use color slide film and let the owner choose which transparency he or she wants printed. If black-and-white film is preferred, have a "contact sheet" made and let the owner choose from that.

Some tips: Carry a wire grooming brush for last-minute pet touch ups. Get acquainted with the pet first, and have the owner present. Choose familiar-to-the-pet surroundings and an uncluttered background. A light-colored animal looks best against a dark-colored background, and vice versa. Avoid shadows. Use a pet's favorite toy to divert its attention. (Don't use an edible toy unless you know the pet is trained to sit or beg before receiving a treat.) Photograph the pet in a variety of poses.

Set your fee for each customer according to the cost of film and developing, and add a percentage of that amount for your profit.

And hope it rains cats and dogs!

—Mary Joyce Porcelli, Norfolk, Virginia

PIE SOCIAL AND FACE AUCTION

To raise funds for our ever-empty youth coffers, we held a Pie Social and Face Auction. You can do the same.

We designated five mothers of kids in our youth group to get 35 to 40 individuals to each bake or buy and donate one pie. The pies were to be used for the social scheduled after a Sunday evening worship service.

We then asked all the board members and deacons to donate their faces for the face auction to be held during the pie social. We required the youth pastor and senior pastor to be involved in the fun too.

The youth group purchased Styrofoam cups, paper plates, plastic forks, Dixie cups, ice cream, coffee, whipping cream and pie tins. Group members prepared many whipped cream pies for the face auction.

For $1.50, each person received a slice of the pie of his or her choice, coffee and a Dixie cup filled with ice cream.

The face auction was quite a hit. We had an auctioneer, chosen from the congregation, who really helped drive up the prices of the faces. (One board member's face sold for over $100!) The highest bidder got to throw a whipped cream pie into the face purchased.

In an hour and a half, we raised over $700.

—Randy Gross,
Sioux Falls, South Dakota

71

POPPING FOR PROFIT

With a few donations and minimum effort, popcorn can puff up huge profits for your youth group.

If some parents are critical of popcorn as junk food, just ask, "What is more natural than corn?" If you use a hot-air popper and no salt or butter, all those crispy little fluffs in that four-cup bag add up to about 100 calories.

Borrow two or three electric poppers, and ask people to donate butter-flavored salt, small paper sacks and lots of popcorn.

Obtain permission from a school principal to sell popcorn on the campus every day after school for a week (or every Friday for a month).

Ask for volunteers to publicize the event at the school. Arrange a regular time and place to pop popcorn and bag the goods. Then set up a rotating schedule to be sure everyone gets a chance to be involved.

Go ahead and try this fund-raising project. You'll have a lot of fun while you produce 100 percent profit!

—Linda Hazzard, San Diego, California

SMALL AMOUNTS COUNT

Here is an easy, profitable fund raiser. Remind your youth group that if every member gives a little, it helps the total a lot.

Give each group member a plastic dime container. (We paid 20 cents each for ours.) Most coin or hobby stores sell the containers. Ask your young people to contribute two dimes a day for 20 days for whatever project you choose. (We selected our youth budget, but the money could go for anything.) When the containers are collected, emptied and the dimes counted, the money will make a significant contribution to your project.

We also asked the congregation members to join us. They were enthu-

siastic. Again, emphasize that when everyone pitches in, a
lot can be accomplished.

—Rev. Don Immel, Elkhart, Indiana

SOUPER SUNDAY

Our youth group wanted to serve a meal as a fund raiser.
We also discussed Super Bowl Sunday as a possible date
for the event. Our discussion led to soup as our entree item
and the selection of the name Souper Sunday.

If you want to use this fund-raising idea, hold Souper
Sunday on Super Bowl Sunday and feature four kinds of
homemade soup (for instance, chicken noodle, beef vege-
table, chili with beans and split pea with ham), tossed salad
with choice of three dressings, dinner rolls and coffee, tea
or fruit drink. Charge $3 for adults (free refills of soup in-
cluded) and $1.50 for children under 12. Sell large brown-
ies for 25 cents each. Shop carefully to find the best buys
on items for the meal. Youth group members eat free **after**
all others are served.

Start the fund-raising publicity three to four weeks before
the event. Design a sign-up poster with a football Souper
Sunday theme and place it on a church bulletin board.

Youth group members and sponsors meet early in the afternoon for food preparation and table-setting. Seat customers at tables. Have some of the youth group members act
as waiters, taking orders and delivering food to tables; the
others serve as the kitchen crew.

Encourage church members to bring portable television
sets so everyone can watch the game easily. You might
want to borrow or rent a large-screen television to add to
the event's excitement. Serve popcorn during the game.
Provide board games and other activities for those who
aren't football fans.

One benefit of this fund raiser: It helps group members
develop a ''servant spirit.'' Preparing, serving and cleaning
up after the event and waiting to eat until everyone else is
served helps develop this servant quality.

—Randy and Naomi Martin, Tacoma, Washington

SUMMER CHRISTMAS AUCTION

Try this fun fund raiser! Though not a new idea, it's been successful for many groups.

First, enlist a local auctioneer who will be a good sport and dress up like Santa. Then set your date, sometime during July or August—preferably on a 25th.

Canvass local stores for donations of new items to be auctioned. Tell the store managers what your group is doing, and that at the auction you'll advertise the stores that donated the items. Attach a 3x5 card with the merchant's name on each item while it's on display. And have the auctioneer mention the store each item is from before auctioning it.

Whether you hold your auction indoors or outdoors, decorate with all the Christmas trimmings—tree, lights, garland, mistletoe, nativity scene, wrapped gift boxes, etc. Play Christmas music in the background. Serve Christmas cookies and punch for refreshments. And don't forget a treat for all the kids from Santa!

—Barry French
Damascus, Ohio

THE GREAT SALAD BAR EXPERIENCE

Here is a fund raiser that is easy to coordinate and is mostly profit. Here's how it works.

● Several weeks before the event, make a sign-up sheet for group members to choose which salad bar items to bring. Include soups, bread, Jell-O, toppings, dressings, lettuce, paper plates, cups, etc., and suggested amounts.

● Announce the event and ask adults to also sign up to contribute some of the salad bar items on the list.

● If needed, you can buy extra items at reduced prices if you explain the fund raiser to grocery-store managers.

● Write reminders for those who have signed up to bring their items before the morning worship service on the designated day. Ask some of the teenagers to help you set up the salad bar and wait on "customers" after the service. Choose one group member to collect the set fee or donations.

Every time we have sponsored The Great Salad Bar Experience we have raised from $75 to $150.

—Don Immel, Elkhart, Indiar

TRASH-A-THON

Had a Trash-a-thon lately? While not a new idea, it is always worthwhile.

Young people get sponsors per bag of trash they will collect, up to 10 bags. Have them ask for a minimum of 25 cents per bag. They can go door to door in the community too; we found that people were eager to support us when they realized how they'd benefit from the project.

When the day arrives, turn your young people loose in pairs in parks, neighborhoods, and other areas that need clean-up jobs. After group members have finished their collections, they report back to their sponsors on how many bags they filled with trash, and then collect the money.

All of our kids filled 10 bags, and we raised enough money to pay for our entire beach trip.

And the community looked a lot nicer!

—Aaron K. Price, Haw River, North Carolina

VALENTINE HEART CAKES

Here's a new twist on an old, familiar valentine treat.

You've probably seen the small, candy hearts with cute sayings on them that most stores sell around Valentine's Day. Our youth group took that idea, reworked it a little and came up with personalized heart-shaped cakes.

Three weeks before our great valentine-cake bake-off, we took orders for the cakes from the congregation. Having good-looking samples to show really helped our sales. We charged $3 for small heart cakes; $5 for larger ones. (Each cake cost us less than $1 to bake and decorate.) The person who bought the cake got to add his or her own personalized message that would appear on the cake.

On the weekend before Valentine's Day, the youth group met at the church to bake, decorate and personalize the cakes people ordered. The young people responsible for baking the cakes used large and small heart-shaped pans. A person who decorates cakes professionally taught the kids to decorate cakes neatly and with a creative flair. Finally, we added the personal messages. Of course, we made extra cakes without messages to sell to last-minute cake buyers. For a small fee, youth group members delivered the cakes.

We earned $110 after paying expenses. Actually, we got a lot more than money from this fund raiser. We had a great time working together, learning new skills and seeing all the smiles when people received the heart cakes with the special messages.

—Alan Muck, Paducah, Kentucky

76

WEIGHT AWAY

There are many fad diets to help people lose extra pounds. Here's an idea that not only helps others lose weight but raises money for your group as well.

For six weeks we conducted a fund raiser called Weight Away which is similar to the Weight Watchers program. Those who take part pay a $3 entry fee and weigh in once a week, usually before or after church. Each time they weigh they pay $1.75. An added incentive: Each person must pay $1 for every pound he or she gains during that week.

Provide sample diet and information booklets on health and nutrition for each person who enrolls. Sample diets and helpful booklets are available from most weight clinics, health clubs, health food stores, local physicians or from the local library. Encourage participants to exercise.

Materials you'll need:
- Scales (preferably a doctor's scale)
- Notebook to chart each person's weight loss/gain (keep the information confidential)
- Small gift (to be awarded to the person who loses the most weight)

Set up a room in your church for this fund raiser. Publicize the event a few weeks before it starts. Stress the importance of having as many people as possible to participate. You may also want to serve fruit juices while people weigh in.

We earned over $100 with this fund raiser. People had fun losing weight, even if it was only for a short period of time.

—Mitzi Rowland, Seth, West Virginia

YOUTH GROUP STOCKHOLDERS

To raise money for our group's mission trip to Mexico,

we invited adults (18 or older) to invest in the youth group by becoming stockholders.

This simple idea, passed on to us by Reverend Ed Light in Enid, Oklahoma, generates enthusiasm among adults—and money in the youth fund.

First we got a plain stock certificate from a stockbroker in town. We copied the format and adapted the language to suit our own purposes.

For six weeks we publicized this opportunity and sold stock at $10 a share. (Solicit involvement from non-church adults by running a news release in your local newspaper, telling why you're raising the money.) All stockholders received official-looking certificates documenting their support.

Upon our return from the trip, we sent all our stockholders invitations (with RSVPs) to a banquet run by the youth group. Each share was worth one free admission. We showed slides of our trip, talked about our experiences, and gave our supporters a special thank you.

We sold 180 shares, and after the dinner we figured we had netted $1,600 that was used toward the trip.

—Kirk Dana, Bartlesville, Oklahoma

YOUR IDEAS WANTED

Have you participated in a fun, original youth group activity? **GROUP** Magazine is on the lookout for creative, unique youth group games, parties, retreats, discussions, special events, worship ideas and fund raisers.

If your group has an idea, submit it to the following address:

"Try This One"
GROUP Magazine
Box 481
Loveland, CO 80539

You will receive a check for every idea we publish.

OTHER MINISTRY RESOURCES FROM

DENNIS BENSON'S CREATIVE BIBLE STUDIES, BY DENNIS C. BENSON. This huge resource offers 401 complete, creative Bible studies for ALL of Matthew, Mark, Luke, John and Acts. 660 pages. $19.95.

COUNSELING TEENAGERS, BY DR. G. KEITH OLSON. The authoritative, complete, and practical reference for understanding and helping today's adolescents. Hardbound, 528 pages. $19.95.

GROUP MAGAZINE'S BEST YOUTH GROUP PROGRAMS (Volume 1). A massive collection of the 79 BEST Bible studies, meetings and other practical programs from GROUP, the youth ministry magazine. 224 pages. $17.95.

THE YOUTH WORKER'S PERSONAL MANAGEMENT HANDBOOK. Provides unique help for youth workers as they seek to better control and manage their professional and personal lives. Hardbound. $16.95.

THE GROUP RETREAT BOOK, BY ARLO REICHTER. This is *the* resource for start-to-finish retreat planning, execution and evaluation . . . plus 34 ready-to-use retreat outlines. 400 pages. $15.95.

YOUNG ADULT MINISTRY, BY TERRY HERSHEY. How to build a successful ministry with those in their 20s and early 30s. $12.95.

SPIRITUAL GROWTH IN YOUTH MINISTRY, BY J. DAVID STONE. Offers help for youth workers to grow in their relationship with God. Also offers incredible opportunities for spiritual growth in youth groups. Hardbound. $12.95.

CREATIVE WORSHIP IN YOUTH MINISTRY, BY DENNIS C. BENSON. An ideas-packed resource for youth worship in various settings—youth Sundays, youth group meetings, retreats and camps, many more. $11.95.

BUILDING COMMUNITY IN YOUTH GROUPS, BY DENNY RYDBERG. Offers practical guidance and workable ideas to develop a caring Christian youth group. Over 100 creative activities. $11.95.

VOLUNTEER YOUTH WORKERS, BY J. DAVID STONE & ROSE MARY MILLER. A step-by-step process for involving adults in a vital youth ministries program. $6.95.

STARTING A YOUTH MINISTRY, BY LARRY KEEFAUVER. An insightful book with tips on starting a youth ministry program or revitalizing an existing program. $5.95.

THE BEST OF TRY THIS ONE (Volume 1). A fun collection of games, crowd-breakers and programs from GROUP Magazine's "Try This One" section. $5.95.

MORE . . . TRY THIS ONE (Volume 2). A bonanza of youth group ideas—crowd-breakers, stunts, games, discussions and fund raisers. $5.95.

TRY THIS ONE . . . TOO (Volume 3). Scores of creative youth ministry ideas. $5.95.

TRY THIS ONE . . . STRIKES AGAIN (Volume 4). A gold mine of original, simple and fun youth group activities. $5.95.

Available at Christian bookstores or directly from the publisher: Group Books, Box 481, Loveland, CO 80539. Enclose $2 for postage and handling with each order from the publisher.